300

D1572320

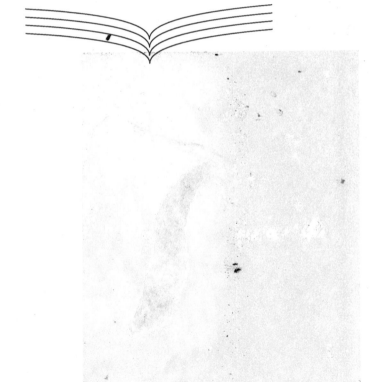

also by Sharon Loeschen

THE MAGIC OF SATIR
Practical Skills for Therapists

THE SECRETS OF SATIR

Collected Sayings of Virginia Satir

Virginia Satir

THE SECRETS OF SATIR

Collected Sayings of Virginia Satir

SHARON LOESCHEN, M.S.W., L.C.S.W.

Illustrated by Susan Green LoNigro

EVENT HORIZON PRESS
LONG BEACH, CALIFORNIA

1991

THE SECRETS OF SATIR
Collected Sayings of Virginia Satir

Frontispiece photograph of Virginia Satir by Jackie Schwartz

Library of Congress Catalog Card Number 91-75154
ISBN 0-9627501-6-6

Printed in the United States of America

First Softcover Printing, September 1991

Published by Event Horizon Press
Post Office Box 14645
Long Beach, California 90803

TO THE MEMORY OF VIRGINIA SATIR

Introduction

I decided to write this book as a way of sharing the wisdom I gained from Virginia Satir, who was a world famous family therapist and social worker. Many refer to Virginia as the "Columbus of Family Therapy" because she discovered the effectiveness of conducting psychotherapy with entire families, as opposed to the traditional method of working with one individual at a time.

In 1979, I watched Virginia work with families at a workshop in Springfield, Illinois. I was very impressed with her knowledge, skills, and most of all, her loving way of being with people. Then in the spring of 1986, I watched her work with couples at a workshop in Los Angeles. Again I was impressed and I decided I wanted to study with her.

That summer I went to Virginia's month-long training, which she called a "process community," held high up in the Rockies of Colorado. Most of the ninety participants were counselors, but there were also teachers, physicians, homemakers, musicians, and ministers. The training was the most growth producing month of my life—so much so that I decided that I wanted to go back the next summer for further training. I am very grateful for that decision, because Virginia died the following June.

The book is a collection of Virginia's sayings—or as I prefer to call them, her "secrets." Virginia discovered many of the universal principles of how and why people behave the way they do, and she shared these during her trainings. The opportunity to gain her "secrets" firsthand was lost with her death, so I decided to share the ones I have collected through this book.

I chose the word "secrets" for the title not only because of her discoveries about how we humans operate, but also because

Virginia was famous for helping families to get their own "secrets" out in the open and deal with them. Virginia believed that freedom of expression is the key to an emotionally healthy family, and that "secrets" create barriers to expression.

I have organized her sayings under five major headings: families, self-worth, communication, feelings and change.

The book can be read in any fashion that suits your fancy. You may read it sequentially, jump around, or read a page at a time.

I hope you find it of value.

Sharon Loeschen

Long Beach, California
August 1991

Acknowledgments

I want to acknowledge these people for their tremendous help in bringing this book into existence,

- Bob Loeschen, my wonderful husband, who fully supported me in taking the time, money and energy to study with Virginia; also for his patient and constructive editing of my many rewrites;

- Harris and Mildred Parsons, my parents, who gave me a loving, nurturing environment in which to grow and blossom;

- Becky Thorn, who has been a marvelous support and critic of my writing;

- Ruth Williamson-Kirkland, who sent me many messages of encouragement to help me get through the month-long trainings with Virginia in Colorado;

- Sirri Hanson, who nurtured and guided my growth to the point that I had the courage to take the risk to study with Virginia;

- Joan Brown, who suggested that I create a separate work of Virginia's sayings;

- Jackie Schwartz and Judy Weinstein, who helped me get my creative juices flowing;

- Dee Abrahamse, who patiently listened and supported me through the many hurdles;

- Dianne Ramstead who gave me her feedback;

- Sharon Olson, who enthusiastically helped with the format and editing; and

- Susan Green LoNigro, who did the magnificent drawings for this book—so beautifully capturing the feelings of Virginia's sayings.

Collected Sayings of Virginia Satir

Section I — Families

Section II — Self-Worth

Section III — Communication

Section IV — Feelings

Section V — Change

I — Families

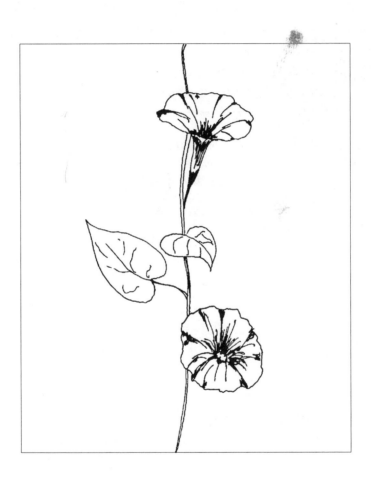

" **F** *amilies are systems,*
and all living systems
go toward balance."

Virginia first discovered that our families work as systems
when she was working as social worker in a mental hospital in
Chicago. She was treating a young woman and she noticed that
just as the young woman starting getting better, her mother got
deeply depressed and her father had a heart attack. She also
noted that when these events occurred in the family, the young
woman got sick again. Virginia concluded that these changes
were not coincidental and that she needed to treat the family as
a system—as a whole.

When we change our behavior, we may experience strong pulls
from our family to go back to our old ways of being. We have
upset the balance of the system and the system will try to right
itself by pressuring us to return to our former behavior.

When we understand the nature of systems, we can resist the
pressure to return to our previous ways of being. We can become
the person we want to be.

*"**T**here are two kinds of systems:
open and closed."*

Virginia determined that all systems, including families, can be
open or closed based on their ability to respond to change.

When we have a closed family system we tend to be

- inflexible about the rules,

- unclear about what the rules are, and

- secretive.

When we have an open family system we tend to be

- flexible, changing the rules
  as the children's needs change,

- clear about what the rules are, and

- up front with what is happening
  in our family.

"*C hildren are like seedlings— they grow best when they are in a nurturing environment.*"

Virginia believed that often we create unnurturing environments for our children by assuming:

- that in marital and parental relationships, someone must dominate and someone must submit,

- that to be different from others in the family is bad,

- that when there is a problem, one person has to be at fault, and

- that it's best to avoid change and preserve the status quo.

She also believed we are very capable of change, and that we can change our families to nurturing environments by:

- seeing the members of our families as equal in personhood, regardless of age or gender,

- celebrating our personality differences, our uniqueness,

- understanding that our problems are multicausal and not needing to find fault, and

- accepting and celebrating change as the way of nature.

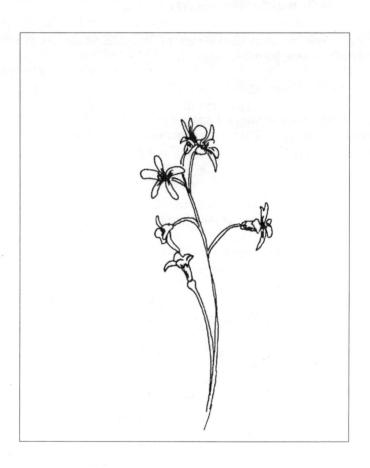

" *T* *he key to a healthy family*
is a happy marriage."

When children were referred to Virginia for help, she would begin her assessment by looking at the health of the parents' marriage. Virginia believed that children are greatly affected by what is happening in the marriage.

When our children see us in pain and unable to resolve it, they too will be in pain. They may express their pain in a variety of ways such as:

• wetting the bed,

• being aggressive with other children,

• being hyperactive,

• performing poorly in school,

• under- or over-eating,

• having nightmares,

• having difficulty sleeping in their own beds, or

• turning to drugs or alcohol in their teens.

When our children see us treating each other with respect, communicating openly and being able to work out our differences, they feel more secure.

" ***W*** *hen each person in a couple has a center, both will feel of value, and the relationship will be enhanced.*"

For Virginia, to have a center meant to have a sense of identity and wholeness, of completeness in and of oneself. Often, however, we have been taught to look to our partners for a sense of completeness. For example, women have been taught to look to men for leadership, and men have been taught to look to women for nurturance.

When we enter a relationship with such expectations, we often become disillusioned. We may be unhappy and blame our partner for our unhappiness, not realizing the inappropriateness of our expectations.

As we are able to become aware of and let go of our expectations, we will be able to let go of our disappointment in our partner. In addition, as we are able to call upon our undeveloped parts, we will feel better about ourselves and more complete.

"*C onflict is unavoidable because
it is a manifestation of our differentness.*"

Virginia assumed we will have conflicts in our families, because each of us is a different person with a different perspective.

When we pretend that we don't have conflicts, we often develop psychosomatic illnesses. The pain of the conflict is felt and held in our bodies, making us sick.

When we accept conflict as a normal part of life, we can deal with it openly. We can even look forward to it, knowing that we can learn and grow from it.

"**W**omen learn from their mothers
how to parent and from their fathers
what to expect of a husband.
Men learn from their fathers
how to parent and from their mothers
what to expect of their wives."

Virginia believed that the model we had from our parent of the same sex influences how we are as a parent. She also believed our experience with our parent of the opposite sex affects our expectations of how our spouse would and should be.

If we are not aware of these principles, we may

- feel disapproved of by our partner because our parent was disapproving;

- feel disappointed in our partner because we had been disappointed in our parent's ability to meet our needs;

- feel controlled because our parent was controlling; or

- feel abandoned because we were physically or emotionally abandoned by our parent.

When we understand that we bring expectations into our marriage from our past, we can look for them. We can talk about them. We can work on letting go of them.

" **Y** *ou can't teach something you don't know.*"

Virginia believed that if we weren't taught how to be emotionally healthy, it is hard for us to model this for our children.

When we

- fight over who is right,

- stuff our feelings or explode,

- get down on ourselves when we fail,

- work all of the time,

- have difficulty disciplining ourselves, or

- use substances to help us cope,

our children will tend to do the same.

When we can

- learn to negotiate and accommodate,

- learn to release our feelings appropriately,

- accept our failures,

- discipline ourselves, and

- allow time for play,

our children will do the same.

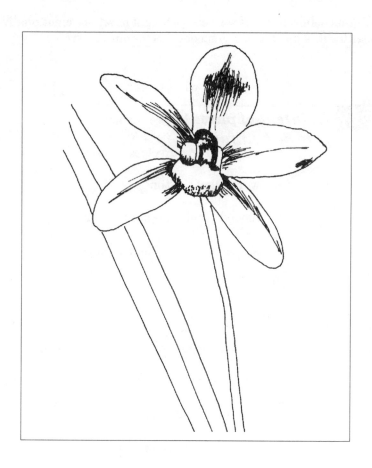

" **T** *he intent of parents
is to be helpful to their children.*"

Virginia believed that we want to be good parents. We want to be helpful to our children, even though oftentimes we don't know how.

When we as parents are having difficulty with our children, we may blame ourselves. We may feel guilt or shame and not be able to ask for help.

When we can give ourselves credit for good intentions, we can be more forgiving of our humanness. We may also find it eaier to seek information, guidance, or support for ourselves.

" *T he emotional honesty of parents with children is more important than any specific technique."*

Virginia believed that being straight with children is the foundation of effective parenting.

When we are dishonest with our children about what is really going on for us, our children may have difficulty trusting their own perceptions. They see one thing but are told something else. They become confused, sometimes to the point of not trusting themselves. Children will always assume they got it wrong. They will never conclude their parents are mistaken.

When we are dishonest with our children, they may have difficulty trusting others as well as themselves. They may approach the world from a distrusting place. This is not healthy. We need to teach our children how to be discriminating—but basically, they need to be able to trust.

"*A child is an intruder for the parents.*"

Virginia recognized that when we have a child, the relationship that we had prior to the child's birth has been intruded upon. She believed that this fact needs to be acknowledged and dealt with.

When we as parents deny or can't talk about the changes we go through with the addition of a child, we often experience tension. The tension comes from holding back our feelings. We may even start fights with each other as an attempt to relieve the tension.

When we can acknowledge and talk about our problems in adjusting to having a child, we are more free to love. We don't have to use our energy to hold down negative thoughts and feelings.

"**W**e often put hats on others *that don't belong to them.*"

Virginia used the image of "hats" as a way of helping people understand that we often attribute characteristics of our parents or other relatives to our spouses or children.

We may see our child as being stubborn simply because he has a nose similar to Uncle George and Uncle George was stubborn. We may resent one of our children because he or she reminds us of an ex-spouse.

We may accuse our spouse of being controlling, because one of our parents was controlling. We may feel abandoned by our spouse, because we were abandoned as a child.

It can be extremely helpful to remove the "hats" we have on family members that don't belong to them. We create the opportunity for new beginnings.

"*A ll children are geared toward expression. If they are not expresing themselves, they have been stifled by family rules.*"

Virginia believed that all families have unspoken rules that children learn about how they are to be. She identified five rules that she felt are common in families and especially destructive to our children's self-worth.

The five rules she identified are:

- "It's not okay to express myself—
to say what I think and feel."

- "It's not okay to see and hear
what is really going on in my family."

- "It's not okay to feel what I feel."

- "It's not okay to ask for what I want."

- "It's not okay to take risks."

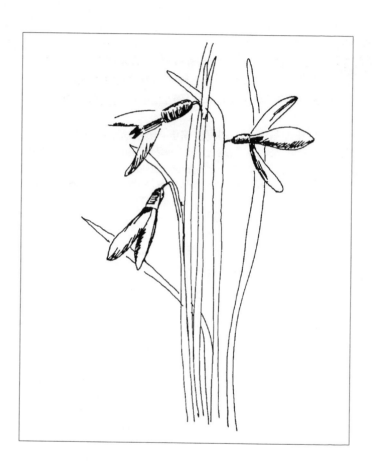

"*A ll children know what is going on, but don't necessarily have a voice for it.*"

Virginia once told a story of being called in by a hospital to help treat a baby who was vomiting uncontrollably. The physicians could find no physical reason for the vomiting. Virginia determined that the baby must have been picking up tension between the parents. She suggested that they hold the baby between them while she worked on their relationship. The baby stopped vomiting.

When we as parents assume that our children are too young to perceive our pain, we may ignore physical or emotional signs that they are hurting.

When we as parents understand that our children are capable of picking up what is happening with us, we can be more alert for signs that they are in pain. We can reassure them that they are not the reason for our pain. We can reassure them that we will take care of them, and that they do not have to take care of us.

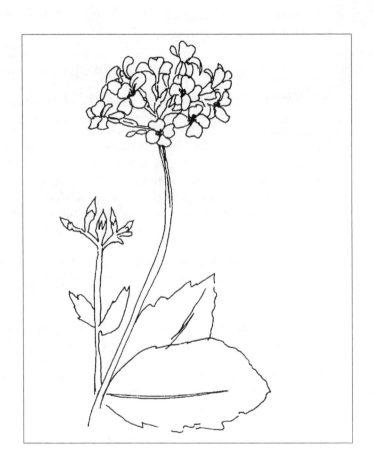

"*C* hildren are willing to sacrifice themselves for their parents, always.*"*

Virginia believed that our most basic instinct is to survive. As children, we equate our survival with the survival of our family system. Because of this, we will do or be whatever we sense our family needs, in order to insure its survival. This may not be who we really are.

We may:

- sense our mother's need for support and become her counselor, even though we are not ready to handle it emotionally;

- intuit that the family needs glory and become an over-achiever, driven to achieve, but without satisfaction;

- feel the need our brothers and sisters have for nurturance, and become their caretaker, even though we have not had that need met in ourselves.

As we become aware of the ways in which we sacrificed ourselves for the sake of the system, we can begin to change. We can let go of roles or old ways of interacting which are no longer useful to us.

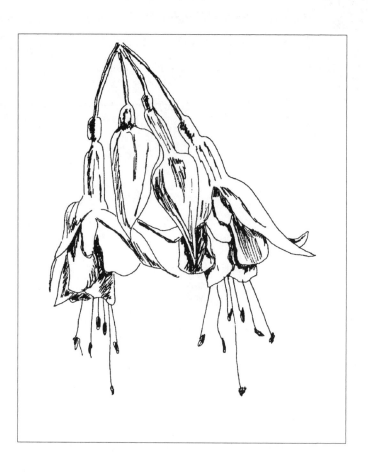

" ***T**he beliefs that made it possible for us to live—may keep us from living.*"

Virginia used the terms, "beliefs," "family rules" and "survival messages" all interchangeably. She believed that as children we behave according to our family's rules or beliefs in order to survive. These beliefs should be blessed for helping us survive, but some may be hindering us now in terms of our ability to express ourselves or interact effectively as adults.

When we find ourselves

- unable to feel or unaccepting of our feelings,

- reluctant to take risks, stuck in our fear,

- hesitant to share our thoughts and feelings,

- unaware of our wants or frightened to ask for them, or

- denying what is going on around us,

we are probably carrying beliefs from childhood.

When we become aware of our beliefs, we can decide which ones are keeping us from living more fully. We can practice being a different way, despite a belief that says it's not okay. We can reassure ourselves that we are no longer children needing to follow a particular rule in order to survive.

"*All children are first-born. There is the first second child, the first third child, and so on.*"

Virginia noticed that when we perceive ourselves as "the second child," we may also perceive ourselves as second best.

She believed that our world is created by our perceptions, and that we can create negative perceptions when we label our children according to the order of their birth.

When we refer to our child by such labels as "my middle one," "daughter number three," or "our baby," we are creating a perception for ourselves and our child which is depersonalizing.

When we as parents can recognize the uniqueness of each child and relate to the child based on his or her personality rather than birth order, we help to create a sense of worth.

" *A little protection never hurt anyone.*"

Virginia believed that children need to be protected by their parents. They need protection to survive. They also need protection in order to have a sense of psychological safety. When children feel safe, they are more likely to have a high sense of self-worth.

When we acquiesce to teachers at the expense of our children, we are not protecting them. When we acquiesce to our spouse at the expense of our children, we are not protecting them. When we acquiesce to family or community pressure at the expense of our children, we are not protecting them.

When we can gather our courage and stand up for our children, they will be benefited.

"We can fully contact only one other person at a time."

When Virginia wanted to give her complete attention to someone, she would sit or stand squarely in front of the person, often holding both of the person's hands. Virginia noted that we cannot be squarely in front of two people at the same time.

As parents, we may find ourselves feeling frustrated in trying to give attention to more than one child at a time. We may also find our children feeling cheated and acting demanding.

When we understand the principle that we can only give our full attention to one other person at a time, we may take more care in the way we position ourselves to listen to our child. We may also take time to reassure our other children that they will be attended to later.

"**W**e learned as children that we should look up rather than across."

Virginia believed that a healthy relationship between parents and children means one in which the feelings and thoughts of the children are considered to be just as important as those of the parents. She recognized that children need limits and believed these can be set without the negative use of authority.

When our children experience us as controlling or threatening, they often grow up to be adults who are overly accommodating or overly defiant to authority figures.

When our children experience us as respectful of their thoughts and feelings, they are more likely to become adults who are at ease with people in positions of authority.

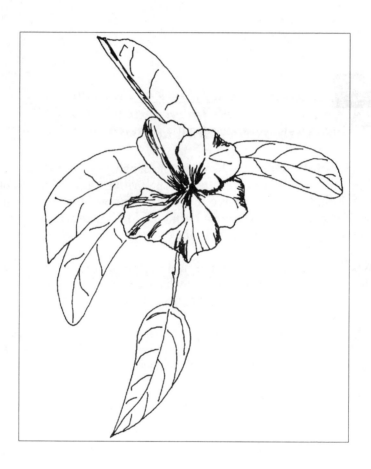

"*C hildren see only parts of their parents.*"

Virginia developed a therapeutic intervention called "family reconstruction." This is a process where a group will re-enact segments of a person's family history, such as the childhoods of their parents, and their parents' courtship. One of the purposes of the intervention is to help people see their parents more fully, to gain a greater understanding of them.

When we view our parents solely from the view we had of them as children, we tend to be more blaming. We often lack empathy for their deficits. We may see them in terms of black or white, leaving no room for gray.

When we as adults can look at the lives of our parents as having been children and young lovers, we often see them in a much different light. We may be able to appreciate their strengths more easily and have a greater understanding of their weaknesses.

"**W**e need to appreciate the *five-year-old within each of us.*"

Virginia recognized that as adults we still carry with us many of the beliefs, feelings and unmet yearnings from our childhood. She felt that if we can realize this, we can be more understanding and accepting of ourselves. We can also be more nurturing to ourselves.

We are appreciating the child within us when we are

- comforting ourselves when we are frightened or hurt;

- asking for help when we need it;

- acknowledging our fear of being vulnerable;

- allowing time for play; and

- talking kindly to ourselves when we make mistakes.

*"*__T__*here is a difference between*
the pain of blame and
the pain of recognition."

Virginia believed that we can become stuck and not grow if we are blaming our parents for the way they raised us. She believed that for growth we need to be able to recognize our pain, feel it, and then look for ways to make things different for ourselves.

We are stuck in the pain of blame when

- we bring up the same complaint about our parents over and over;

- we keep hoping they will change;

- we resist changing our attitude toward them.

We are in the pain of recognition when

- we see the limitations of our parents;

- we feel the impact of their limitations;

- we know that the only person we can change is ourselves.

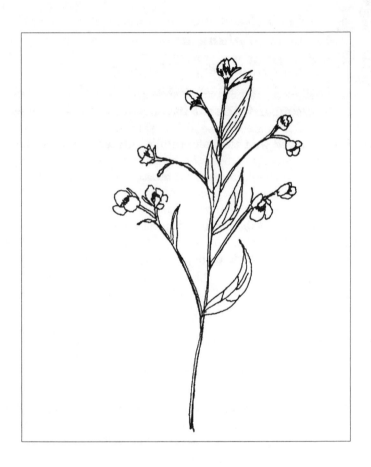

" ***A*** *sperm and an egg got together to create us, so we all started out as part of a triangle."*

Virginia believed that the concept of triangles in a family is a very important one. When the first child is born, the first triangle is created. With each additional child, the number of triangles increases geometrically.

Virginia taught that we need to understand the complexity that is added with each child in terms of the number of triangles. She also believed that triangles can contribute to the strength of a pair, but most of us see a third person as taking away from a pair. We have believed the old adage that "two is company and three is a crowd."

Virginia viewed triangles as offering greater stability than is possible with a pair, just as a tripod provides more stability than something that is two-legged. She also saw triangles as offering greater possibilities for nurturance and feedback than is possible with just a pair.

"*T*riangles consist at any one time of an activator, a responder, and an observer.*"

Virginia identified the activator as the one who is speaking, the responder as the one listening to the speaker, and the observer as the one who is taking in the interaction of the activator and the responder.

Virginia saw triangles as providing the possibility for the role of observer, and she considered that a great addition. The interacting pair has someone who can give them feedback about their interaction. She used this concept a lot in her work, asking one member of a family to give observations of how two others were interacting.

We can use this concept as well. When we are in conflict with someone, we can ask an observing third person to give us feedback about our interaction.

"W *e are all made of parts, only one of which is foreground at a time."*

Virginia saw us as having many different parts to our personality. She believed that we need all of our parts in some form. She believed that the more we know, accept, and manage all of our parts, the more whole we will be.

Some of our parts are:

our powerful part .... our vulnerable part

our intelligent part .... our stupid part

our helpful part .... our selfish part

our sexy part .... our prudish part

our nurturing part .... our critical part

our honest part .... our dishonest part

our loving part .... our cruel part

When we interact, sometimes our parts clash. For example, when one of us has our sexy part out, the other's prudish part may be out. Or when one of us has our vulnerable part out, the other may have the critical part out.

As we can allow more of our parts to surface, we will have more awareness and control of them. We will also have more energy and resources at our disposal.

"_T he world is a family of nations._"

Virginia traveled around the world demonstrating family therapy. As she did, she began to see similarities between the problems of families and the problems of nations. These are:

- the concentration of power in one person or role

- the pressure for conformity and obedience,

- the use of blame, and

- the use of threat, force and violence.

With this realization Virginia felt hopeful, because she believed we can create greater peace between our family of nations just as we do with families, by learning to

- communicate honestly and clearly,

- cooperate rather than compete,

- empower rather than subjugate,

- enhance individual uniqueness rather than categorize,

- use authority to guide and accomplish, rather than for gaining compliance,

- love, value, and respect each other,

- be responsible to each other, and

- use our problems as challenges and opportunities for creative solutions.

II — Self-Worth

" **S** *elf-worth is the crucial factor
in terms of what happens inside
and between people.*"

Virginia believed that the level of our self-worth is the key to how we feel and how we behave. She was trained in psycho-analytic theory, which works on the premise that the key determinants of our behavior are our sexual and aggressive drives. However, after years of experience in treating people with emotional and behavioral problems, Virginia concluded that self-worth is even more of a determinant.

She noted that when we are experiencing low self-worth, we are more likely to behave in destructive ways—either toward ourselves or toward others. We may hold on to negative beliefs about ourselves, creating the possibility of depression, anxiety, or defensiveness. We often get involved in hurtful relationships. We are more likely to be addicted to harmful substances or harmful activities.

On the other hand, Virginia noted that when we are experiencing high self-worth we behave in more mature, productive and loving ways. We can see ourselves as worthwhile even when we make mistakes. We can take risks. We are able to choose and maintain supportive relationships. We have creative energy and a desire to contribute to society.

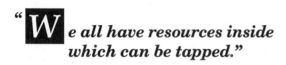

" **W** *e all have resources inside which can be tapped.*"

Virginia believed that one of the many ways to increase our level of self-worth is to use more fully the inner resources that we have been given.

She identified our inner resources as such things as our abilities

    to explore,
            imagine,
                  feel,
                       see,
                           hear,
                                express,
                                        ask,
                                          act,
                                              and choose.

Virginia also believed that courage and wisdom are inner resources which can be tapped.

"**W**e all have the ability to choose."

The ability to choose was a resource that Virginia continually emphasized. Her belief was that the more we exercise our ability to choose, the more empowered we will feel. And vice versa, that the more empowered we feel, the more we will see the many choices available to us.

When we are not feeling good about ourselves, we tend to see ourselves as prisoners of life with few choices. We feel trapped and helpless, believing that we are stuck with whom we are, where we are, or what we have. And we are more likely to see problems as having a limited number of solutions.

When we are feeling better about ourselves, we can see more solutions, more choices. We are more open to new ways of thinking and being.

" **H** *igh self-worth means being able* ✓
to respond to people but not be
defined by them."

For Virginia, the more we are able to feel good about who we are, the more we are able to make decisions based upon what seems right for us. We are able to hear the opinions of others, but we are not bound by them.

Conversely, the more we are able to decide and act upon what seems right for us, the better we will feel about ourselves.

"*P*eople are unique, and therefore impossible to compare.*"*

Many of us have been given the message that "to be different is bad," that it is not okay to be different from others. We have believed it. Virginia saw this message as being very destructive to our self-worth.

To her, the miracle of life is that no two of us on earth are exactly alike, that we are each unique. It is impossible, therefore, for us to compare ourselves.

We can, however, celebrate our unique contributions to the world.

"**R** *ejection is an issue of self-worth.*"

For Virginia, it is a matter of low self-worth when we perceive ourselves as being rejected.

She believed that when we are not feeling good about ourselves, we are more likely to see exclusion as a matter of rejection. If we are not invited or included, we tend to think there is something wrong with us.

When we are feeling worthwhile, we are comfortable with the fact that sometimes we fit in with a particular group or situation and sometimes we don't. We understand that it is a matter of fit, not worth.

" **P** *eople tend to respond to others*
as they think of themselves."

It was Virginia's belief that the way we act toward others is directly related to our feelings about ourselves, our level of self-worth.

When we do not feel good about who we are, we are more likely to see others negatively and to be critical and unaccepting of them.

As we are able to think more positively of ourselves, however, we are more able to be accepting of others. As we can accept our own mistakes, we can more easily accept those of others.

**"*T*he problem is never the problem.
It is our coping with the problem
that is the problem.*"***

It was Virginia's philosophy that there will always be problems,
that they are part of life. To her, the critical issue is what kind of
coping skills we have for dealing with our problems.

Virginia believed that the greater our self-worth, the better our
coping will be. Correspondingly, the more coping skills we
develop, the better we will feel about ourselves.

For Virginia, coping meant

- being able to communicate clearly,
  directly and specifically;

- being able to communicate feelings
  honestly and respectfully;

- being able to use our inner resources
  such as our creativity;

- being able to be open to new learning;

- being able to see change as
  an opportunity;

- being willing to make changes
  and take risks.

" ***T*** *here is a yearning behind every defensive stance.*"

Virginia believed that when we have low self-worth, we have deep unmet yearnings as well as beliefs that we are not okay— that we are covering by defensiveness.

These yearnings may be to be

- wanted,

- loved,

- recognized,

- nurtured,

- approved of,

- accepted.

If we can become aware of our defensiveness, we can also become aware of our yearnings behind the defensiveness. What is it that we are really longing for?

We often still hold the impossible dream that we are going to get that need met by our parent. We need to let ourselves feel the pain of the loss that that will never happen. We can then move on to the work of letting go of that hope and looking for more realistic ways of getting our needs met.

"S *elf-worth is behind every defensive stance waiting to be reborn."*

Virginia believed that the way to help people be less defensive is to help them raise their level of self-worth.

She identified four common ways that we get defensive.

These are:

- placating, when we are
  overly accommodating and pleasing;

- blaming, when we are quick to
  accuse someone else of being at fault;

- intellectualizing, when we get
  super-reasonable; and

- distracting, when we try to
  divert the focus.

For Virginia, underlying each of these defenses was the same belief—that we are not okay.

She believed that the more we can feel okay about ourselves, the less we need to be defensive. Conversely, the less we are defensive, the better we will feel about ourselves.

III — Communication

" **C** *ommunication is to relationships*
what breath is to life."

For Virginia, effective communication is vital to a healthy
relationship.

When we are not communicating with each other effectively, we
often make incorrect assumptions about what the other is
thinking and feeling. We may withhold our true thoughts and
feelings or be unclear about them. We often don't feel heard or
understood and conclude that we are not loved. We may become
depressed and look to others outside the relationship to meet
our needs.

When we are communicating more effectively, we are able to
share our thoughts and feelings and to examine our
understanding of the other person. We are open to learning.

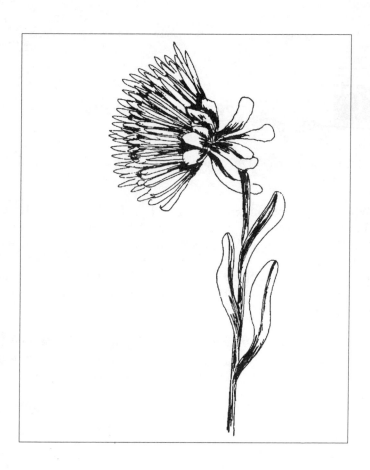

Communication

"*C*ongruence is the mark of *healthy communication.*"

To Virginia, "congruence" meant having our behavior match our feelings. In other words, that we are able to be honest about what we feel. It also means having a high level of regard for others and ourselves.

Virginia pointed out that sometimes we show little regard for others by using a blaming style of communication. Other times we show little regard for ourselves by stuffing our own feelings and being overly accommodating in order not to "make waves."

When we are able to be congruent, we are able to share our feelings, needs, and wants. We are also able to listen respectfully to the feelings, needs, and wants of others.

" **T** *he greatest gift one can give another*
is to see, hear, understand and touch them."

Virginia developed a poster with the above saying on it which
has been distributed throughout the world. On the poster is a
beautiful picture of a hummingbird making contact with a
flower. To Virginia, the way we can make contact with each
other is to listen and observe for understanding. We also can
make contact by touching each other in nurturing ways.

When we don't feel listened to or understood, we often feel
cheated. We may resort to blaming, withdrawing, or even "acting
up" in some way in order to get some kind of attention.

As we work toward really listening, seeing, and understanding
each other, we will feel a greater sense of satisfaction in our
relationships. We may also feel a growing desire to be more
giving to each other.

" *W* hatever you perceive is what you believe. Your world is the outcome of what you perceive."

When Virginia listened to people communicate, one of the key elements she listened for was their perception.

She believed that our perceptions—that is, what we see and hear, and the meaning we give to what we see and hear—create our feelings and often the way we experience life.

She taught that the meaning we give to our perceptions is based on our inner beliefs about the way things are. Our inner beliefs, however, evolved out of our unique and limited experience of the world as a child. Although these beliefs were the best conclusions we could come to at the time, they may not really hold true now.

In order to be effective in interpersonal communication, we need to acknowledge that our perception is not reality, but simply our view based on our beliefs. With that acknowledgment, we can begin to become aware of our beliefs and examine their validity. We can ask others if they see the world as we do. We can open ourselves to new ways of thinking.

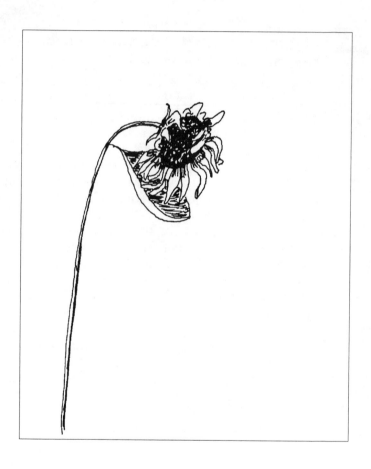

"*C ommunication is with yourself as well as with others.*"

Virginia believed that the way we talk to ourselves is just as important as the way we talk with others.

We often talk to ourselves in very unkind ways. We label ourselves negatively, calling ourselves names like "stupid" or "idiot." We compare ourselves to others and tell ourselves that we are not as good as someone else. We are critical of ourselves, telling ourselves we "should" be different than we are.

Virginia believed that we can change this, and that it is extremely important for our self-worth that we do change it. We can talk to ourselves regularly, telling ourselves that we are valuable, worthwhile, and unique. We can accept our feelings as not right or wrong, but simply our feelings. And we can forgive ourselves regarding our mistakes.

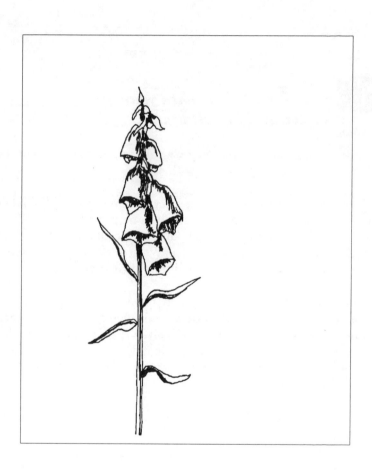

"*M eeting is the beginning of a relationship.*"

Virginia took great care in the way she greeted people. She saw each new meeting as the opportunity to bring the gift of a new person into her life.

When we view the process of meeting as insignificant, we are more likely to treat it lightly. We may even see it as something to "get through," and feel relieved when it's over.

When we view meeting as the beginning of a relationship, we are more likely to take time to reach out and truly see and hear the other. We give ourselves the possibility of adding a new meaningful relationship to our lives.

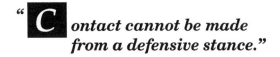

"*Contact cannot be made from a defensive stance.*"

"Contact" was Virginia's word for connection. To her, it is impossible for us to be fully connected with someone when we are defensive. She believed that when we are defensive, our energy is going into protecting ourselves and not into connecting with another.

When we can be open to each other—sharing and listening from a place of caring and honesty—we are more likely to feel connected. We feel respected and equal. We feel validated as separate individuals and at the same time connected in our humanness.

" *I* **ntimacy is your willingness**
to share your truth—with relevance,
appropriateness, and timing."

Virginia believed that initimacy means taking the risk of being honest and vulnerable with a partner. It also means choosing the time and the topic for sharing, based on a consideration of the partner's energy level and capacity to handle what we have to say.

When we disregard our partner's needs and share what we want, when we want, we may hurt the relationship.

When we take our partner's needs into account, we increase our chances of having a satisfying conversation and achieving greater closeness.

" *T* ouching is a universal language. "

Virginia believed that, no matter what their verbal language, all people can understand the language of touch. She also believed that we all need touch. In fact, it was her contention that touch is one of the great unmet needs of most people. Because of this, Virginia touched people a great deal. And she did it in a very caring, loving manner.

She used to say that we can touch with our eyes, our voice, and our bodies.

If we have grown up in families where there wasn't much touching, we may feel uncomfortable with it. But our uncomfortableness does not mean that we don't have a yearning for touch. Unfortunately, there is often a negative correlation between our age and the amount of touch we receive.

If we choose, we can practice getting comfortable with touch.

" ***E** veryone has an invisible skin
about 18 inches out from the body.
Inside this is each person's personal space.*"

Although Virginia was famous for her touch, she also was very respectful and aware of the need people have for space. She observed carefully to see what amount of closeness was acceptable for each individual.

If we are not aware of the body language of others in relation to our closeness, we may cause them to feel uncomfortable—even violated.

When we are respectful of the needs of others regarding space, we are more likely to create a feeling of comfort between ourselves and them.

"**W**<i>hen you meet rigidity,
that's par for the course.
The key is: to not become
more rigid yourself.</i>"

Virginia saw rigidity as a natural defense we use when we feel threatened. She believed that the way to avert further defensiveness is to lessen the threat.

When Virginia was treating someone and they were protecting themselves by being rigid and unbending, she would become softer and more nurturing. She tried not to get hooked into a power struggle.

When we find ourselves being rigid, we can take a look at ourselves and try to figure out why we are feeling threatened.

If we are confronted with someone else's rigidity, we can help ourselves by understanding that it is a protective mechanism. We can stop ourselves from escalating the interaction into a battle for control. We can work on increasing our flexibility.

" ***I*** *n our society, judging*
usually comes before observing."

Virginia believed that most of us jump to conclusions about others much too quickly. Virginia was deaf from the age of five to seven, and during this time she became very astute at observing. She invited people to increase their own observing skills and decrease their judgments.

When we are quick to judge, we often do not see the full picture or we distort the picture. We attribute meaning to the appearances or behavior of others that is based on our own experience, rather than reality.

When we are able to observe without judgment, we often find that our assumptions were not correct.

IV — Feelings

"*F eelings give us our juice!*"

Virginia believed that having access to our feelings is what gives us our energy and our aliveness.

When we are cut off from our feelings, we may feel numb, lethargic, and uninspired. Depression and anxiety may set in. We can even develop illnesses because our feelings are stuck in our bodies.

We find our relationships unsatisfying when we can't relate to the feelings of others.

Virginia helped people get in touch with their feelings simply by asking them frequently how they were feeling. Her belief was that we can learn to be in touch with our feelings by increasing our awareness of them.

When we can develop our capacity to feel, we gain a sense of relief, freedom, and energy. We also increase our ability to empathize with others, which is a very important aspect of being an emotionally healthy individual.

"**W** *hen thought enhances feeling
and feeling enhances thought—
then we have wholeness.*"

To Virginia, we need to be able to use our capacity to feel and our capacity to think in order to be fully human.

When we are over-developed in our ability to think and cut off from our feelings, we are more limited in our ability to experience the many facets of life. We tend to only see and trust facts. We tend to undervalue relationships. Our spiritual needs may get neglected as well.

When we are over-developed in our ability to feel and cut off from our ability to think, we often act impulsively. We can become overwhelmed and immobilized with our feelings. We may tend to see ourselves as helpless and needy.

When we are more in balance, our feelings give us energy and our minds give us the ability to channel that energy into productive ways of being.

" *F* eelings we have in the present
are often generated by
thoughts from the past."

As Virginia saw it, we often have feelings based on previous experiences while attributing them to present ones.

When we are upset with someone in the present sometimes we are really reacting to a reminder from our past. We may see our spouse as controlling because we had a controlling parent. We may be intimidated by our boss because as children we learned to be frightened of authority figures. We may be impatient with our child because he reminds us of ourself as a child.

When we can develop more awareness about ourselves, we are more able to keep clear about what belongs to whom. We are more able to relate to people for who they are, rather than who we think they are.

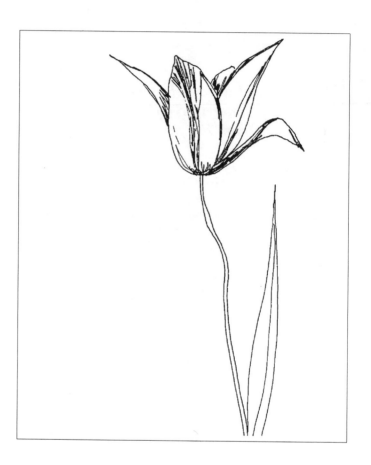

"*F*eelings are merely barometers. They do not dictate our behavior."

It was Virginia's contention that we have grown more and more to believe that we must act on whatever we feel. She disagreed with this way of thinking, inviting us to acknowledge our feelings and then decide if we wish to act on them or not.

When we feel at the mercy of our feelings, we usually don't trust ourselves. We feel a sense of inadequacy. We also tend to be more judgmental of ourselves, believing that we are wrong for what we are feeling.

As we get more in charge of our feelings, we can feel more self-assurance and self-acceptance.

"**F**ear constricts and blinds us."

Virginia observed that when we are frightened we are less flexible and less able to see what is happening around us. We are also often unable to see that we have choices.

When we can acknowledge and accept our fears, we are more able to see new possibilities. We are also more free to act on those possibilities.

Virginia often handed people an imaginary "courage stick," as she called it; that was to be a reminder to them of their inner courage. She would suggest that this imaginary stick was available to them at any time that they needed to "lead with their courage and leave their fear behind."

"*F or every feeling we have, we will have a body response.*"

While working at the Mental Research Institute, Virginia worked closely with physicians trying to understand the relationship of illness to feelings. It was her conclusion that there is a very strong relationship between feelings and illness.

She believed that when we hold on to our feelings, we are increasing our chances of illness. We may hold on to our sadness by not allowing ourselves to grieve a loss. We may hold on to our anger by blaming others. We may hold on to our fear by not sharing it with someone.

When we are able to let go of our feelings, we cleanse our body.

Letting go of feelings can be accomplished by first acknowledging and then accepting them. Once we have done this, we can choose how we want to let go. We can express our feelings, or simply make the decision to let go of them.

"**T**he event is not what we have to deal with—it is the feelings generated about the event."

Virginia believed that our feelings are created by the way we interpret words and behaviors, not the words and behaviors themselves.

She believed this to be a very important concept from the point of view of personal empowerment as well as effective interpersonal communication.

When we do not understand this, we often accuse others of making us have certain bad feelings. We may say, "You made me angry," or "You hurt my feelings." We can feel at the mercy of others. We can also put them on the defensive by our attacking words.

She hoped that we could come to understand that we are in charge of our feelings because we are in charge of our own thoughts and interpretations.

" *A* nger is often a defensive feeling. There are softer feelings underneath which need to be dealt with."

Virginia saw us as having feelings such as disappointment and hurt beneath our protective anger.

When we are feeling angry, we may think this means that we are in touch with our feelings, but often there are other more vulnerable feelings underneath with which we are not in touch.

When we are able to connect with the feelings beneath our anger, we often can get clearer about the source of our pain. We can more easily determine our needs and work to get them met. We can communiate less defensively with others.

"**W**e have feelings about feelings."

One of Virginia's contributions to the process of helping people was to explore feelings about feelings. She discovered that it was often at this level that we get stuck. We carry judgments about the feelings we are experiencing, and these judgments get in the way of their expression or release.

We may carry a message inside that says it's not okay to feel at all. Or we may have judgments about certain feelings. When we feel afraid we may believe that it's not okay to be afraid, and so we get embarrassed about being afraid. When we feel angry we may believe that it's not okay to be angry and so we feel guilty.

When we become more aware of our judgments about our feelings, we can work toward greater acceptance of them. And as we are more accepting of our feelings, we will have greater energy available to us.

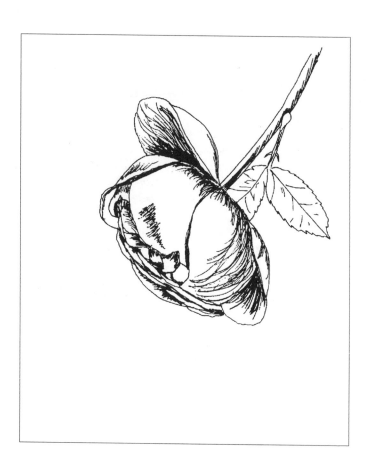

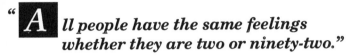 "*All people have the same feelings whether they are two or ninety-two.*"

Virginia believed that we often see children and the elderly as somehow not feeling as much as we do, so we minimize their needs.

When we see children as not feeling as much, we often discount the level of their loss, rage, or fear. This is not only depersonalizing, but also very dangerous because it can lead to abuse.

The same is true for the elderly. When we see them as not having the same kind of feelings as ourselves, we tend to treat them with less compassion and understanding. We tend to discount their needs and their individuality.

We need to understand that we all have the same feelings regardless of our age.

V — Change

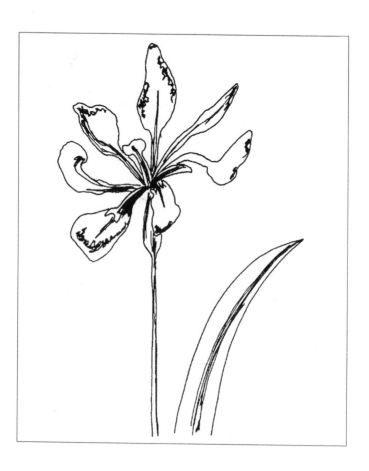

" **P** *eople are capable of change.*"

Virginia saw growth and change as the natural order of the
universe. She believed that we can learn new ways of being no
matter what our age.

When we resist change, it's often because we don't have hope
that things can be better for us. Virginia always had hope and
promoted hope because she knew people are capable of positive
changes. She also knew that we need the energy from hope in
order to change.

Over the years of observing change in people she saw that we go
through univeral stages.

First—we have an awareness that we need to change but
we don't change.

Second—something interrupts our usual way of being such
as a divorce, our child gets into trouble, or we lose our job.

Third—we feel in chaos, distressed and anxious. We are
often in a great deal of pain and feel out of control. We can
go one of two ways. We can choose to stay as we are and
blame someone else for our pain, or we can choose to look at
ourselves and make some changes.

Fourth—if we do choose to change, we come to a new level of
understanding and integration.

Fifth—we must practice the new changes to make them
ours.

Once we understand these stages, we are more likely to be able
to recognize when our pain is really "the stage of chaos." With
this recognition we can feel more in control, and know that we
are at a choice point in the process of change.

"_There is more pull toward the familiar than the unfamiliar._"

Virginia knew that people are capable of change. She also knew that we are drawn to stay with that which we know, no matter how miserable we are, simply because it is familiar to us. We are afraid to change—to go out of the known and into the unknown.

We may continue to placate even though we know it's causing us physical problems, because we fear the consequences of standing up for ourselves. We may continue to be controlling because we have an undefined fear of not being in control. We don't know what would happen and that is terrifying.

We may stay in hurtful relationships—even enduring physical cruelty—because at least it is familiar, we have already experienced it. We don't know what we might have to experience if we were to leave the relationship and go out on our own.

When we can understand our natural pull to stay in the familiar, we can acknowledge it and then, if we choose, we can gather our courage and move into the unfamiliar.

"*T he only real certainty in life is change.*"

To Virginia, the acceptance and use of change for growth was the emotionally healthy approach. She viewed it as unhealthy to try to get security and certainty by resisting natural changes.

When she worked with parents, she looked to see if they were "up to date" and adjusting their expecations for the ages of their children.

We can choose to resist change or acknowledge it and even look forward to it. This is not to say that we shouldn't allow ourselves to feel the losses that go along with changes. But it means we can see change as the way of nature, and the opportunity for greater wisdom and actualization on our part.

"*It is normal to see barriers along with wishes. The problem is when you see the barriers as permanent.*"

In her later years, Virginia's focus was international peace. All of her major workshops ended on the topic of peace. She worked to inspire people from all around the world to work toward peace as well.

In keeping with her belief that we needn't see barriers as permanent, she had been a pioneer in working behind the Iron Curtain, in Eastern Europe, and the Soviet Union.

Unfortunately, Virginia did not live to see her wish for the Berlin wall to come down become reality.

She believed that people are capable of getting rid of barriers and she was right!

" *T* *ake a direction and see if it fits.*
Be aware that your legs can go
forward, sideways, and backward."

Virginia believed we always have choices.

Oftentimes we get depressed because we see ourselves locked into thinking that if we make a change and it isn't the right one for us, we are stuck with it.

Virginia's methaphor was her way of saying that we can change our minds. We can experiment with a change and if it isn't working for us, we can go back to our old way or we may discover other possibilities once we've made the first change.

e can't see our own backsides."

For Virginia, helping people become aware of themselves is the first step in effecting change. She believed that we all have blind spots regarding our own behavior. We can, however, learn about ourselves from others.

When treating a family, Virginia often would say that she had noticed something about what was going on, and ask if they were interested in her observations. In this way, she helped them see their backsides.

Virginia was famous for letting people see her backside. She worked with families in front of professional audiences and then asked for feedback about her work.

We can be helped to see our own backsides by asking our friends, children, partners, bosses, or co-workers how they see us interacting with others.

"***A** wareness releases energy that has been bound up in buried feelings.***"

Virginia would say that trying to keep feelings buried was like trying to keep hungry dogs down in the basement. The longer they are in the basement, the hungrier they get, and the more energy it takes to keep the door shut!

She believed that it was an important part of her role as a therapist to help people free the energy that was being used to hold down feelings.

She therefore focused on helping people become aware of their feelings. She did this is many ways: Encouraging people to breathe deeply as they were having a feeling in order to feel it more fully. Encouraging people to close their eyes and connect with their images as they talked about a significant event in their lives. Encouraging people to notice the sensations in their bodies as they talked about something important to them.

When we can feel our buried feelings in whatever way we find works for us, we will feel released and energized.

**"You don't have to completely let go
of one thing to gain something new.
We can add rather than discard."**

Virginia believed in what she called the "principle of addition" rather than "subtraction" when it came to trying to effect change in behavior. To her, this meant focusing on adding new, more effective behaviors rather than trying to eliminate ineffective ones.

She did not believe in trying to eliminate behaviors because she noted how it often did not work. She concluded that when we focus on eliminating ineffective behaviors, we set up an internal conflict and resistance for ourselves. One part of us tells ourselves we need to stop doing the unwanted behavior, while another part becomes rebellious and wants to do it even more.

When we simply focus on adding new, more effective behaviors, we don't create resistance for ourselves—so changing is easier.

"*H ow we got to be a certain way
is important for our understanding,
but it doesn't fix us.*"

Virginia believed that in order to effect change, we need to
practice new ways of thinking and behaving in addition to
gaining new awareness about ourselves. This differs from the
view of some therapists, who believe that we can change simply
by becoming aware of ineffective behaviors.

Virginia would help people gain new awareness and then provide
opportunites for them to practice new ways of behaving. She
might coach them on how they could be more direct and
straightforward, if their tendency was to please others at their
own expense. She might help a person practice speaking for
himself, if he had a tendency to speak for others. She might help
a person learn how to express the softer feelings underneath his
anger, if his tendency was to blame others.

When we discover something we would like to change about
ourselves, we can practice. We will slip and we will be awkward,
but that's normal. Oftentimes we give up when it comes to
changing ourselves, because we expect to change instantly and
perfectly. But that is not the way we humans operate—we need
time to practice.

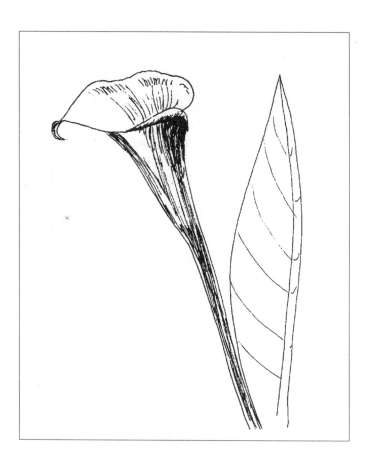

" ***H*** *ealing occurs when you can express
what you knew all the time but
didn't have the words for,
or couldn't express.*"

Virginia believed that when we experience traumas in our lives, we need to be able to express our feelings and thoughts about them. It is through this expression that we obtain release and healing.

Virginia worked to helped people heal from past traumas by encouraging them to reconnect with their images and memories regarding the traumas. She would then explore their feelings— helping the people get in touch with their feelings and talk about them.

Virginia believed that for real change to take place, we need to be able to be in touch with our feelings as well as our thoughts. It is not enough to gain an understanding of what happened to us. We need to feel it and talk about it.

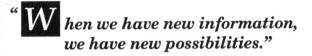

" **W** *hen we have new information,*
  we have new possibilities."

Virginia believed that when we have access to information about the unversal principles of human interaction, we increase our ability to live more effectively.

She saw a major part of her role as a therapist as that of conveying information. She did not give advice but rather shared her observations and understanding of human interaction.

She believed that when we have been given information, we have more choices for how we want to behave and live our lives.

" *R isk is a part of life. It rejuvenates us.*"

Virginia identified the attitude we were taught toward risk-taking as one of the most critical in terms of our self-worth. She believed that when we can take risks, we feel better about ourselves. Similarly, when we don't take risks, we lose respect for ourselves.

Virginia modeled risk-taking. When she began doing family therapy, it was not an accepted method of treatment. She not only took the risk to do family therapy, but she also took the risk to practice it on stage while skeptical professionals watched and critiqued her.

When we can tell ourselves that our success or failure at something new is not related to our basic worth as a human being, we are more able to take risks. The more risks we are able to take, the easier it is to feel good about ourselves.

"*T**ransformation has occurred when a person goes from saying 'I want to be loved' to 'I am loved —by me'.*"

Virginia saw us as having shifted to a place of high self-worth when we can look to ourselves, rather than others, for validation and love.

She believed that once this change has taken place, we are free to

- choose loving relationships,

- take stands for what we believe to be right, and

- focus our energy on productive and creative activities.

ABOUT THE AUTHOR

Sharon Loeschen, M.S.W., L.C.S.W., is well recognized as an accomplished psychotherapist and teacher. She received the 1990 "Recognition for Professional Excellence" Award from Family Service of Long Beach, California. She also received the honor of being selected by Virginia Satir to be a member of the Avanta Network, the organization Satir founded as a way of continuing her teachings.

Loeschen received her Master's Degree in Social Work from the University of Illinois in 1966. Since that time she has had a wide range of experiences as a social worker in Illinois, Iowa and Southern California.

In addition to practicing as a social worker, Loeschen began teaching in 1975 in a systematic counseling skills training program at California State University, Long Beach, under the direction of Dr. Robert Cash. Since then she has taught hundreds of graduate students in effective counseling techniques for individuals, couples and families.

In 1980, Loeschen received her license to practice psychotherapy as a clinical social worker and began an association with Family Service of Long Beach, which she continues to the present.

The Avanta Network, founded in 1977 by Virginia Satir, is an international training organization. Its worldwide members offer training to enhance self-esteem, increase interpersonal communication, and provide a process model for personal and organizational growth. Trainings deepen the participants' understanding of human systems and assist in the process of change.

Avanta-sponsored training events range from week-long to month-long seminars. Members are also available to lead workshops and introduce the Satir model to the public.

For more information, please contact the

        Avanta Network
        139 Forest Avenue
        Palo Alto, California 94301

        415-327-1424.